An Early Career Book

careers at a MOVIE STUDIO

Rivian Bell and Teresa Koenig

photographs by
Gregg Cobarr and
Metro-Goldwyn-Mayer Film Company

Lerner Publications Company
Minneapolis, Minnesota

LIBRARY OF CONGRESS CATALOGING IN PUBLICATION DATA

Bell, Rivian.
    Careers at a movie studio.

    (An Early career book)
    Summary: Describes fifteen possible occupations in a movie studio including producer, director, screenwriter, sound mixer, costume designer, and actor.

    1. Moving-picture industry—Vocational guidance—Juvenile literature. 2. Moving-picture acting—Vocational guidance—Juvenile literature. [1. Motion pictures—Vocational guidance. 2. Vocational guidance] I. Koenig, Teresa, II. Cobarr, Gregg, ill. III. Metro-Goldwyn-Mayer Film Co. IV. Title. V. Series.

    PN1995.9.P75B4   1983   384'.8'023   82-20865
    ISBN 0-8225-0347-6

18046

Text copyright © 1983 by Lerner Publications Company
Photographs copyright © 1982 by Metro-Goldwyn-Mayer Film Company
All rights reserved. International copyright secured. Manufactured in the United States of America.
International Standard Book Number: 0-8225-0347-6   Library of Congress Catalog Card Number: 82-20865

1 2 3 4 5 6 7 8 9 10 92 91 90 89 88 87 86 85 84 83

Would you like to work in a movie studio?

Movies are a wonderful form of entertainment. Sitting inside a darkened movie theater, we can be transported to different times and places—even different planets! Some movies make us laugh or cry; others teach or inspire us. If we like a movie, we often want to see it again and again.

When you watch a movie, you see only the actors. But if you read the *credits,* or list of names, at the beginning and end of a movie, you will see how many people were involved in making it. Most of these people do their work behind the scenes. In this book, you will learn about some of these jobs.

PRODUCER

Before movies can be made, producers must find or create the ideas for the movies. First they find the story to be filmed. Next they must convince the studio to pay for making the movie. The producer is the person responsible for hiring all of the people needed to complete the film, including the directors and the actors.

When the movie is finished, the producer must find a *distributor* who will sell the film to theaters around the country. Producers must be willing to work on the same project for many years. It often takes that long from the time a producer has an idea for a movie until the time the movie is finished.

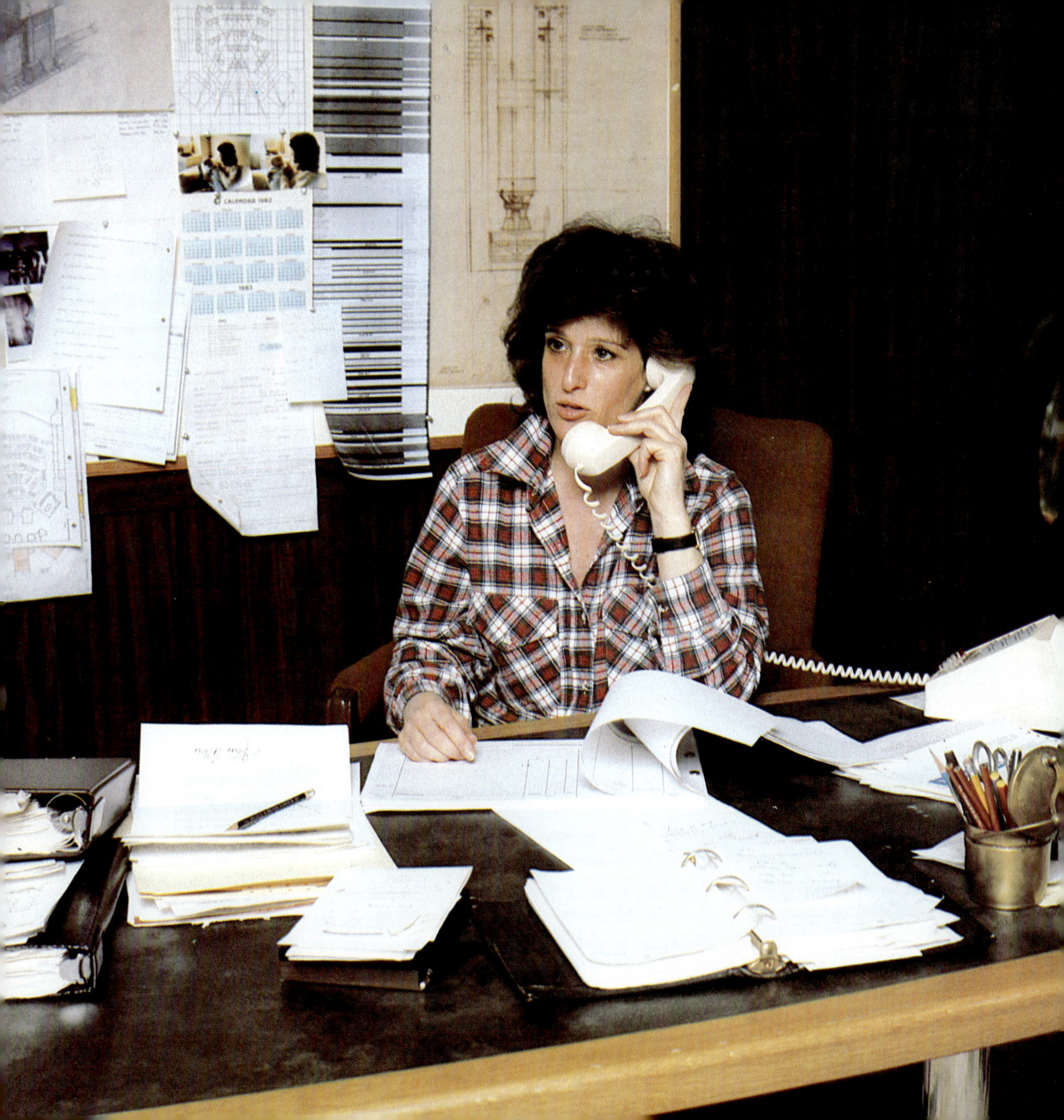
CALENDAR 1982
1983

SCREENWRITER

Screenwriters write the stories for movies. The stories they write, called *screenplays,* contain all of the *dialogue* (DI-a-log), or words, that the actors in the movie will say. They also plan the action and scenes for the movie. Sometimes the stories come from books or from a producer. But often, the story comes from the writer's own imagination.

Good screenwriters understand how people think, talk, and move. They also understand what the camera sees and what the audience wants to watch. Screenwriters are often present while the movie is being filmed.

STOLEN YEARS
MEXICO
CREATION
IBM
WORLD ATLAS
THESAURUS
DICTIONARY

PRODUCTION MANAGER

The two most important duties of the production manager are budgeting and scheduling the filming of a new movie. Movie scenes are usually not filmed in the order in which they will appear on the screen. Production managers use a *production board* like the one in this picture to keep track of when each scene is being filmed and which actors will appear in that scene.

When the production manager knows how long it will take to film the movie, he or she can figure out how much money will be needed to rent equipment, hire crew, and pay the actors. Then, once the filming begins, the production manager must solve any problems that come up during the shooting.

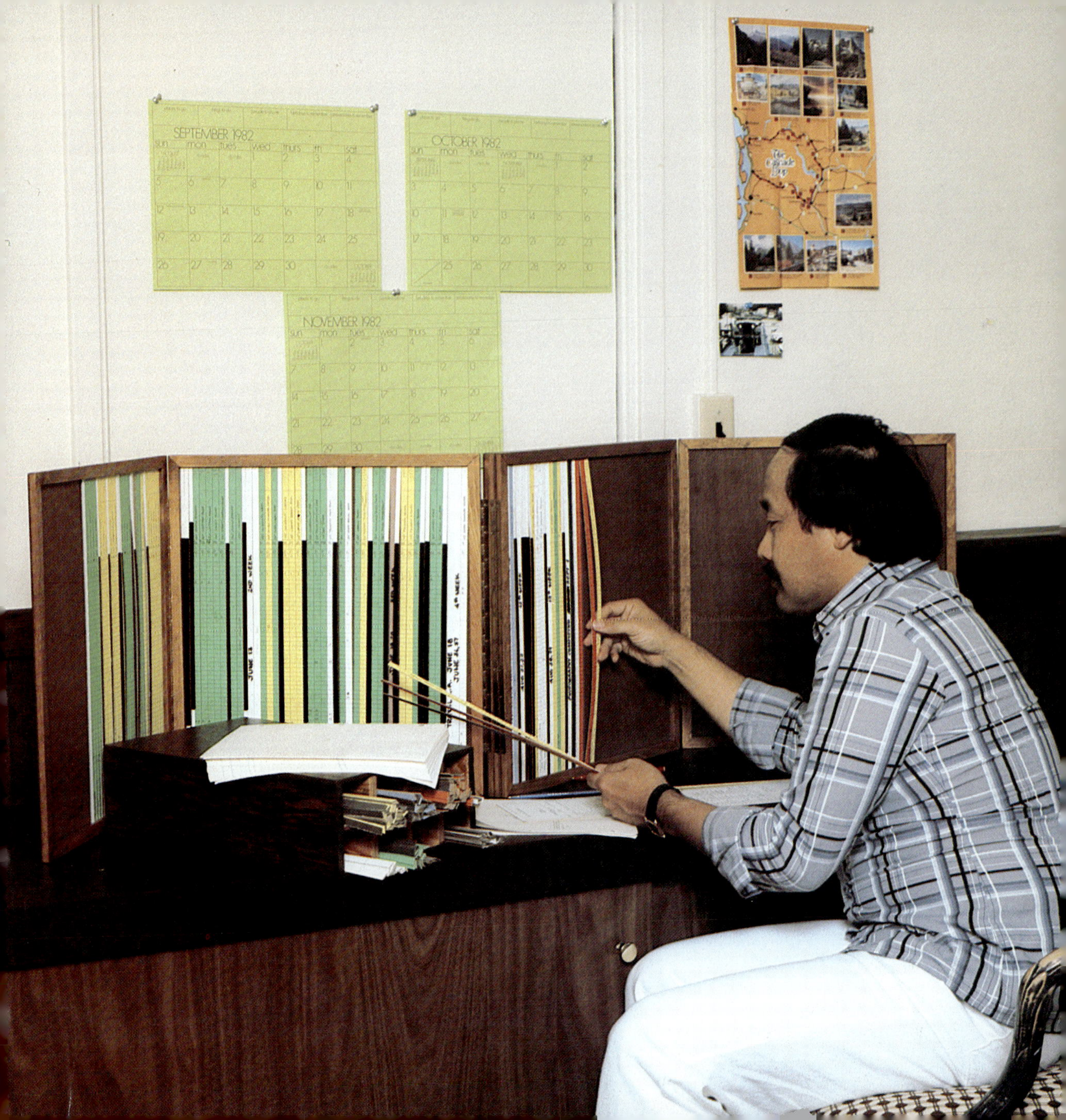
SEPTEMBER 1982
OCTOBER 1982
NOVEMBER 1982

SET DESIGNER

The places where movie scenes are filmed are called *sets*. The set designer's job is to decide what each set will look like. For example, the set designer might want to create an area that looks like a living room. For each set, the set designer must use exactly the right wood, paint, flooring, and windows.

Because building a set can be very expensive, set designers rarely build a whole room. If the camera is only going to see a corner of a room, for example, the set designer will create a set that is only two walls leading to a corner.

Set designers must have an eye for detail. They must make the sets look as realistic as possible.

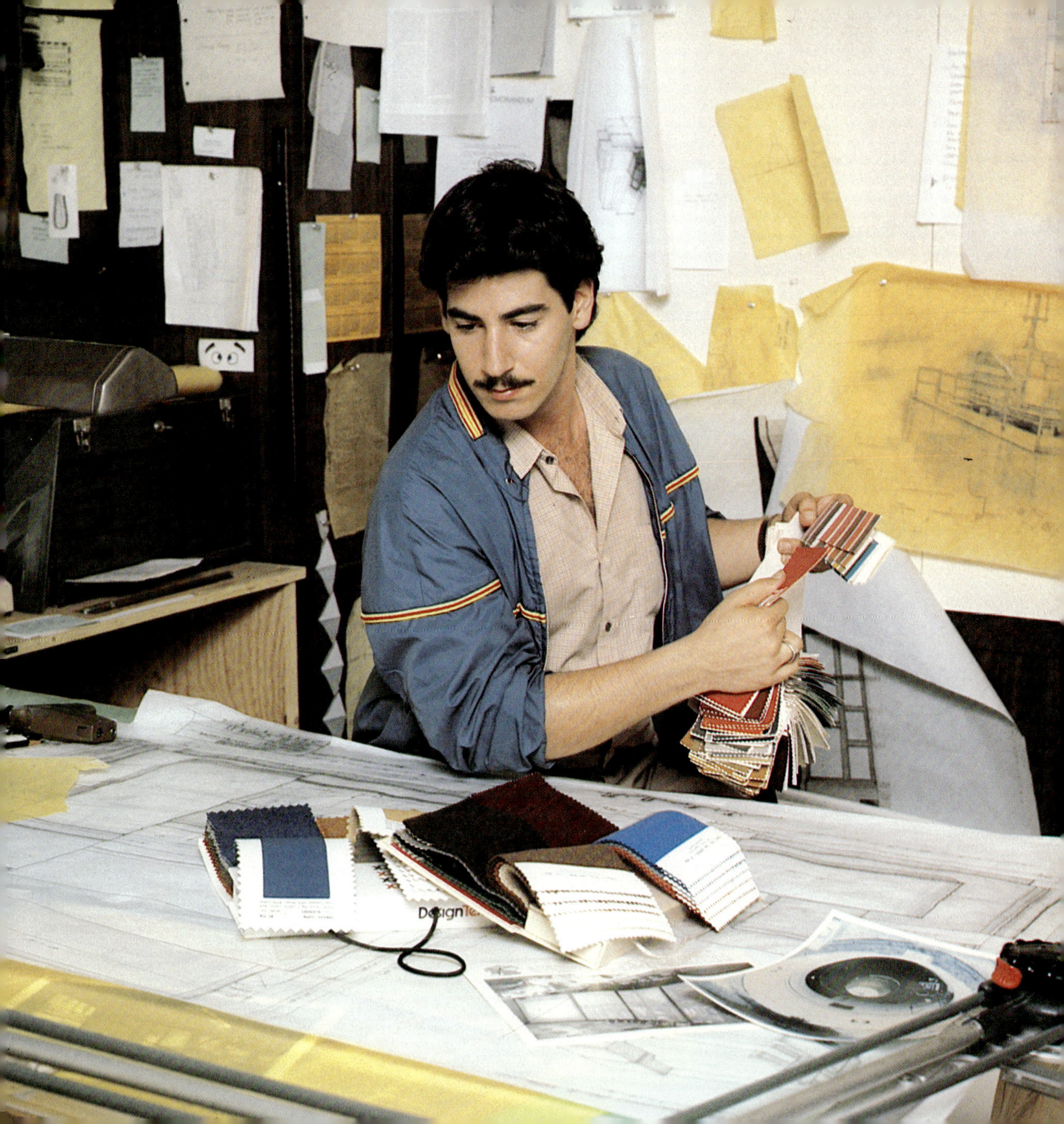

PROPERTY MASTER

To look realistic, a set must be furnished. Every item that an actor uses, from the tables and chairs to the pencils and the telephone, must be chosen. These items are called *properties,* or "props" for short. The person responsible for gathering the right props for each scene is the property master.

The property master reads the script and decides which items will be needed in each scene. Then he or she will often work with the set designer to be sure that the props will fit the style of the set. The studio has a collection of thousands of props stored in a building. This property master is selecting the props for a new movie.

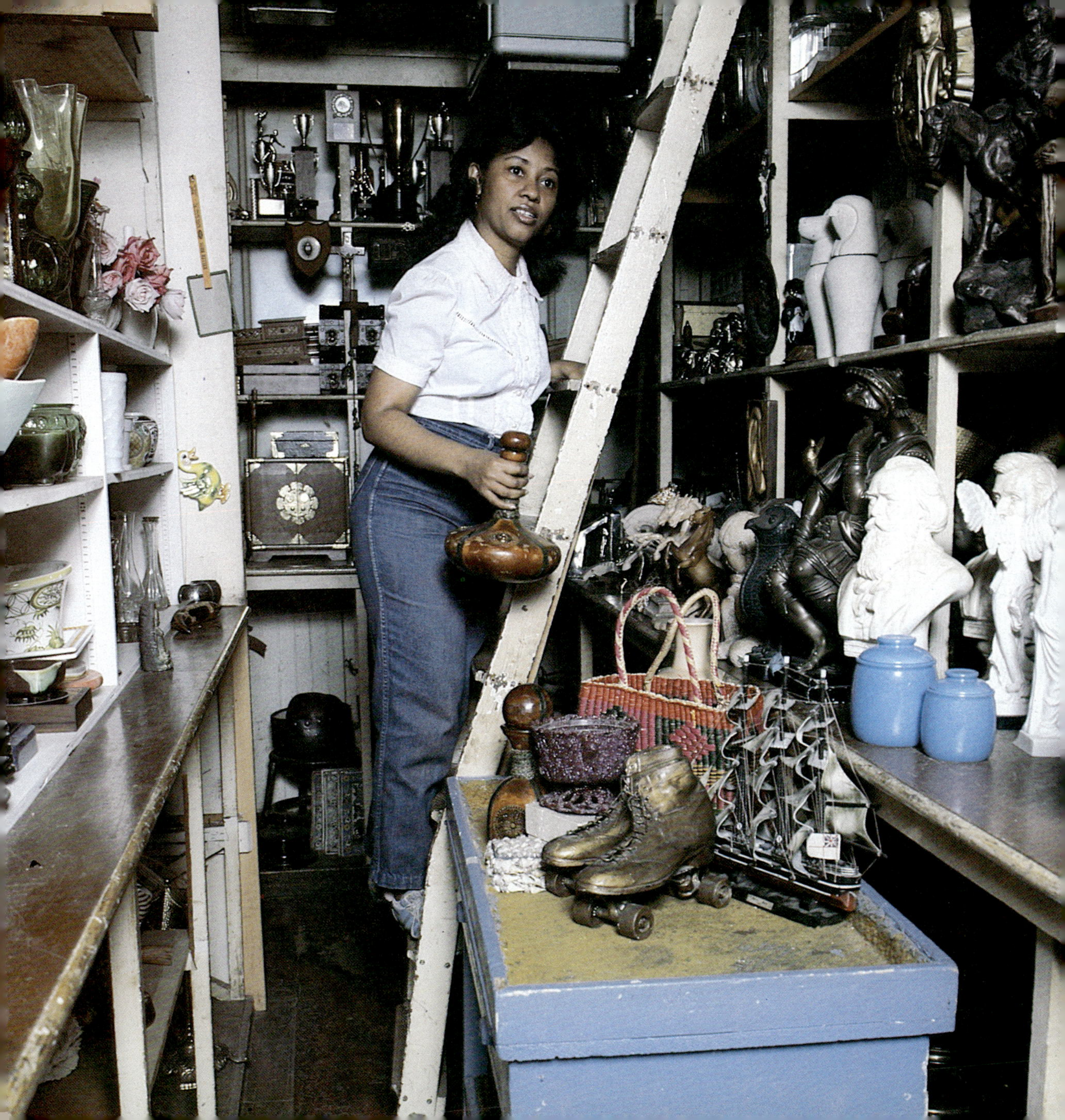

COSTUME DESIGNER

All of the clothes worn in a movie are called *costumes*. The costume designer chooses the style of clothing that best fits the story the movie tells. If the story takes place during the California gold rush, for example, the costume designer must research what style of clothing was worn at that time. For an outer space movie about the future, a costume designer can use his or her imagination to create the costumes.

In this picture, the movie company is filming *on location,* or away from the studio. The costume designer is working in the wardrobe trailer, where the costumes are stored. Here she and an assistant are fitting an actor's costume.

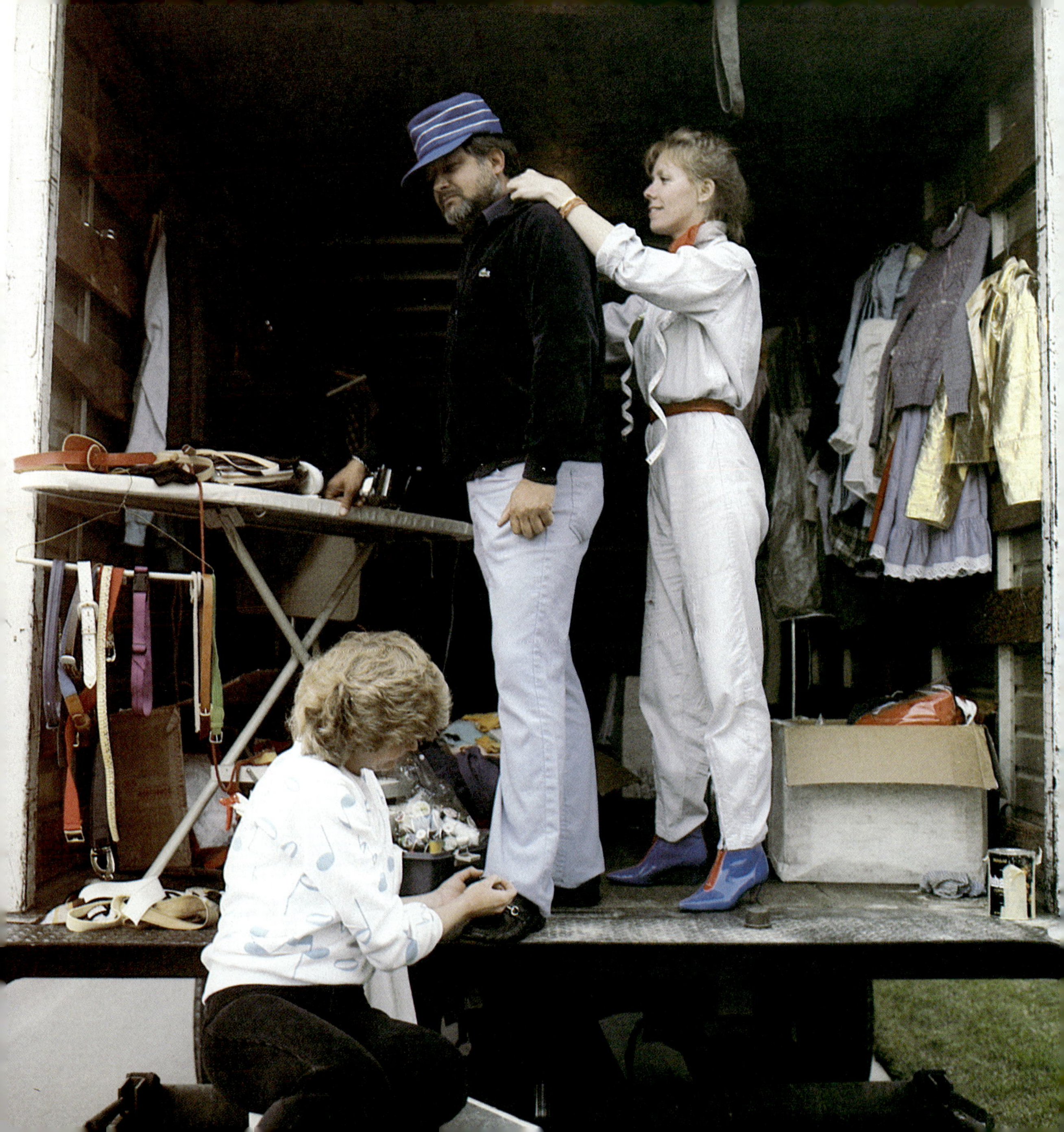

DIRECTOR

Every movie needs a director. The person in this important position works closely with everyone on the production staff, including the production manager, the set director, and the costume designer.

The director's most important job, however, is working with the actors. The director plans each scene and helps the actors to express the feelings of the characters they are playing. Together, the director and actors play scenes over and over again to get the actors' movements just right.

The director also works with the camera people so that the scene is filmed in the best possible way. When all elements of the scene seem just right, the director says "Action!" and the filming begins.

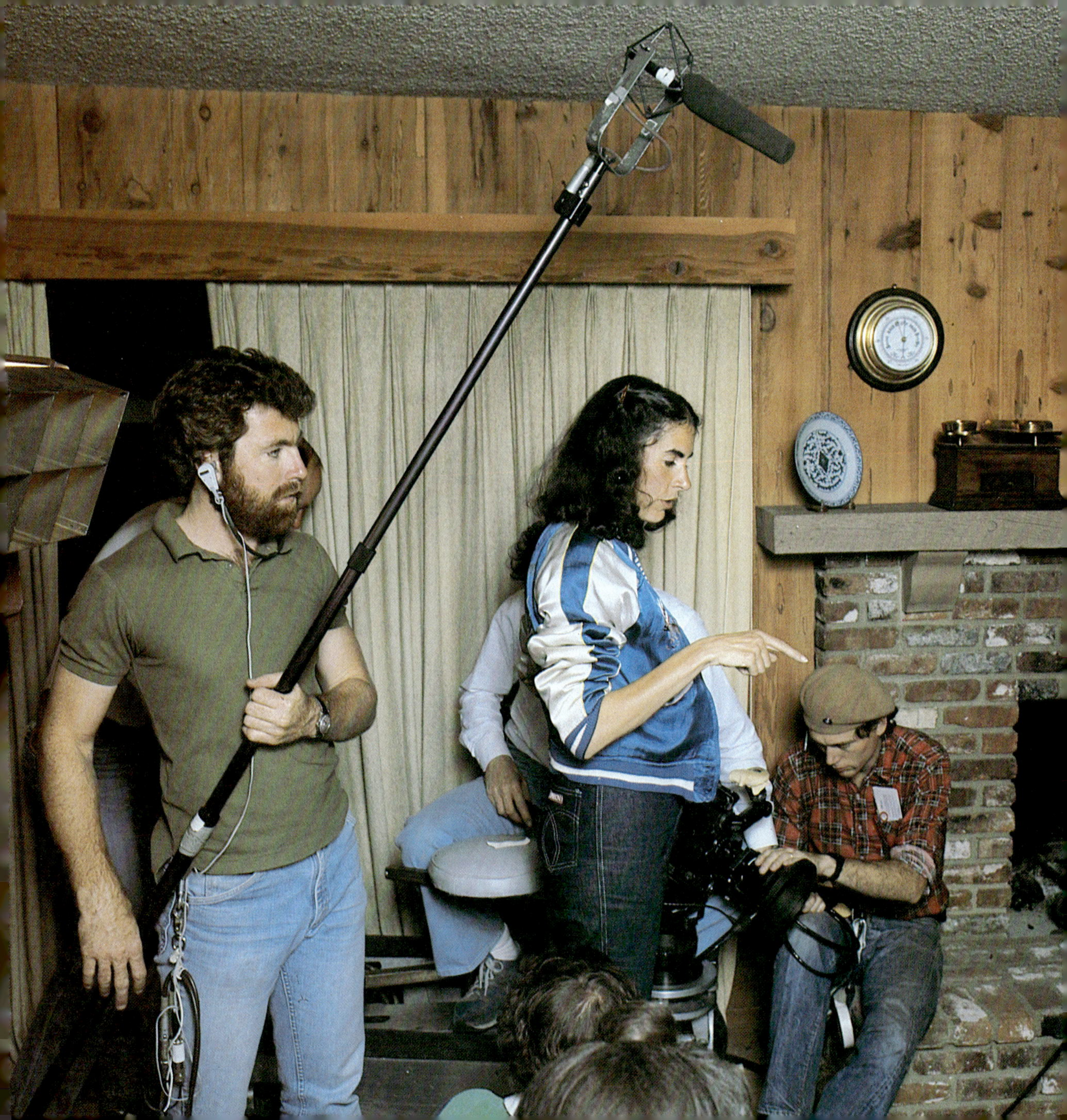

ACTOR

The boy in this photo is a professional actor. Like you, he goes to school, but he also spends many hours rehearsing and learning his lines. All actors must work extremely hard and put in very long days.

Talented actors can make you believe that the characters they are pretending to be are real people. To develop a believable character, actors need many skills. They must express feelings with their voices and their movements. Sometimes an actor must be funny or evil, or must sing or dance. An actor might have an important role and be very famous. Other actors are just beginners and have small "bit" parts or are "extras" in scenes with many people.

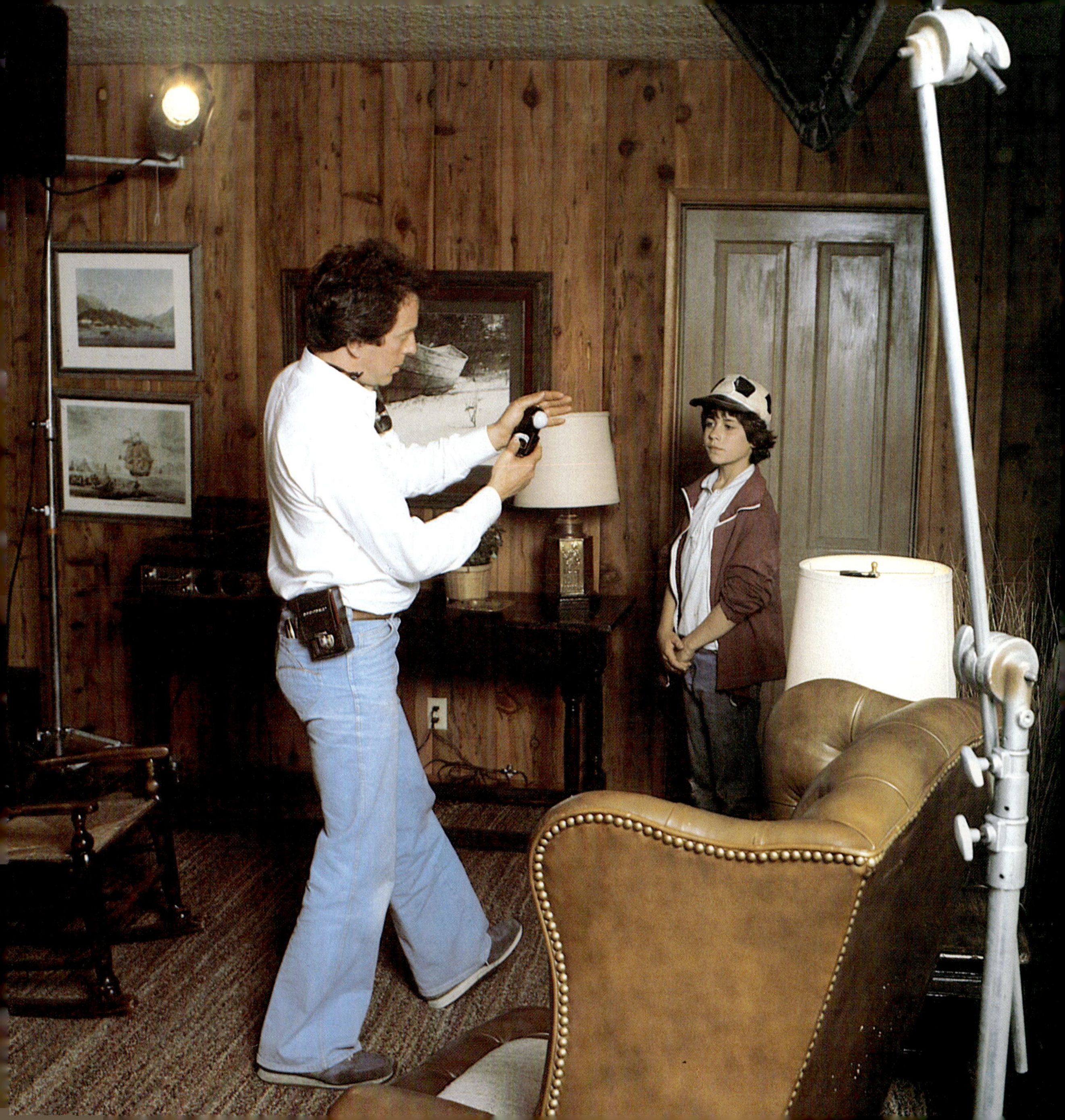

CINEMATOGRAPHER

The cinematographer and the camera crew film the movie. The cinematographer works with the director to decide where to place the camera. Then the cinematographer and the crew *shoot,* or film, the action from different angles.

A movie is often filmed on several different sets. The sets may be indoors on a studio stage, outdoors on a studio street, or on location. For each set, the cinematographer plans the proper lighting, the type of film to be used, and how the camera will move.

A successful cinematographer must know how the motion picture camera works. He or she must also know what makes an interesting picture. The way a movie is filmed often sets the mood for the story.

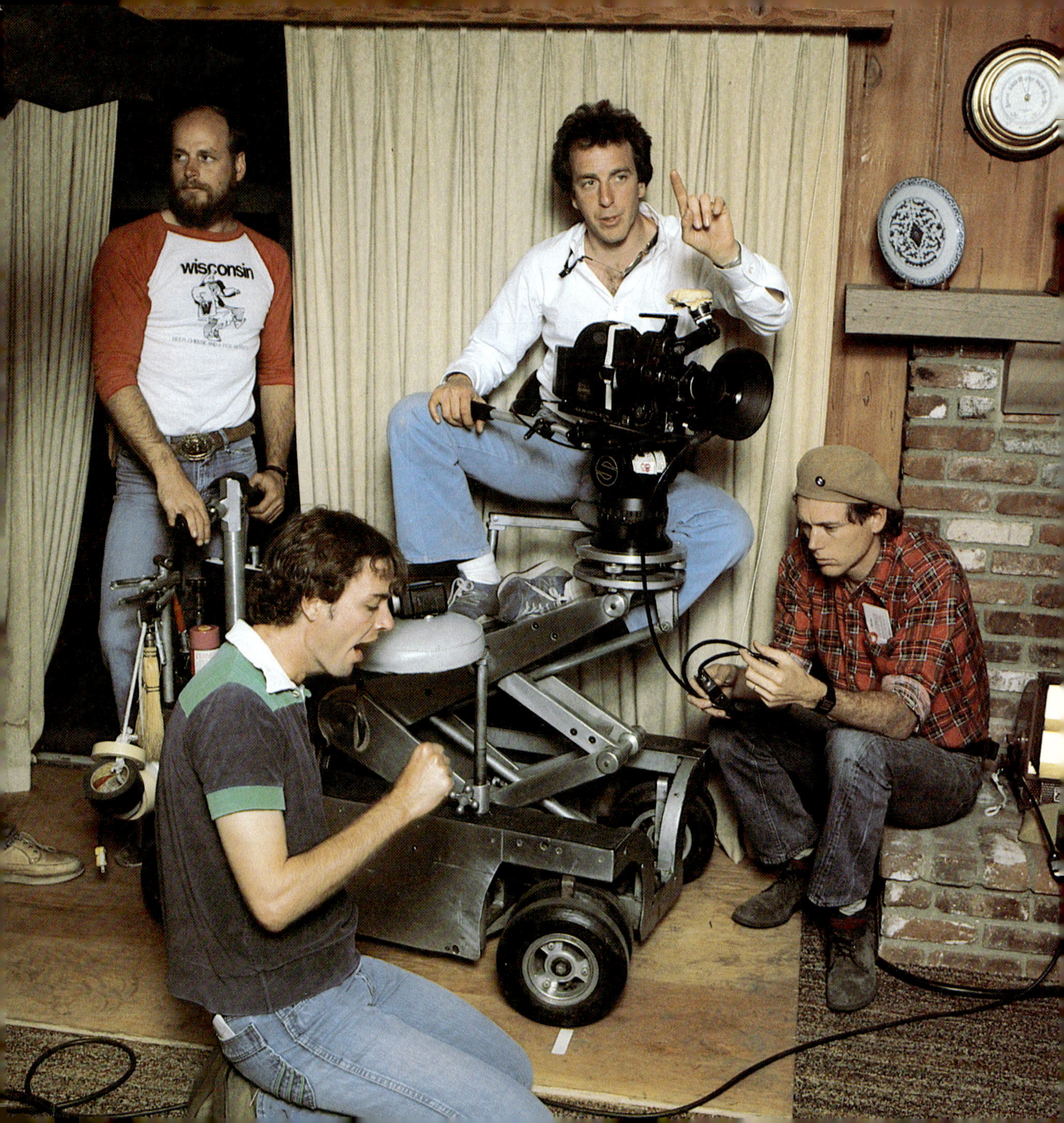
wisconsin

CHIEF LIGHTING TECHNICIAN

The chief lighting technician works closely with the cinematographer and the camera crew. Before the cinematographer can begin filming the action, the set must have enough light on it. Otherwise, the picture will be too dark.

The chief lighting technician helps the cinematographer to create moods and special effects with lighting. This is done by using different colored lights, bright lights, or very few lights, depending on what is happening in the story.

Lighting technicians must know a lot about electricity and lighting equipment. When handling wires, the chief lighting technician wears thick gloves for protection from electrical currents.

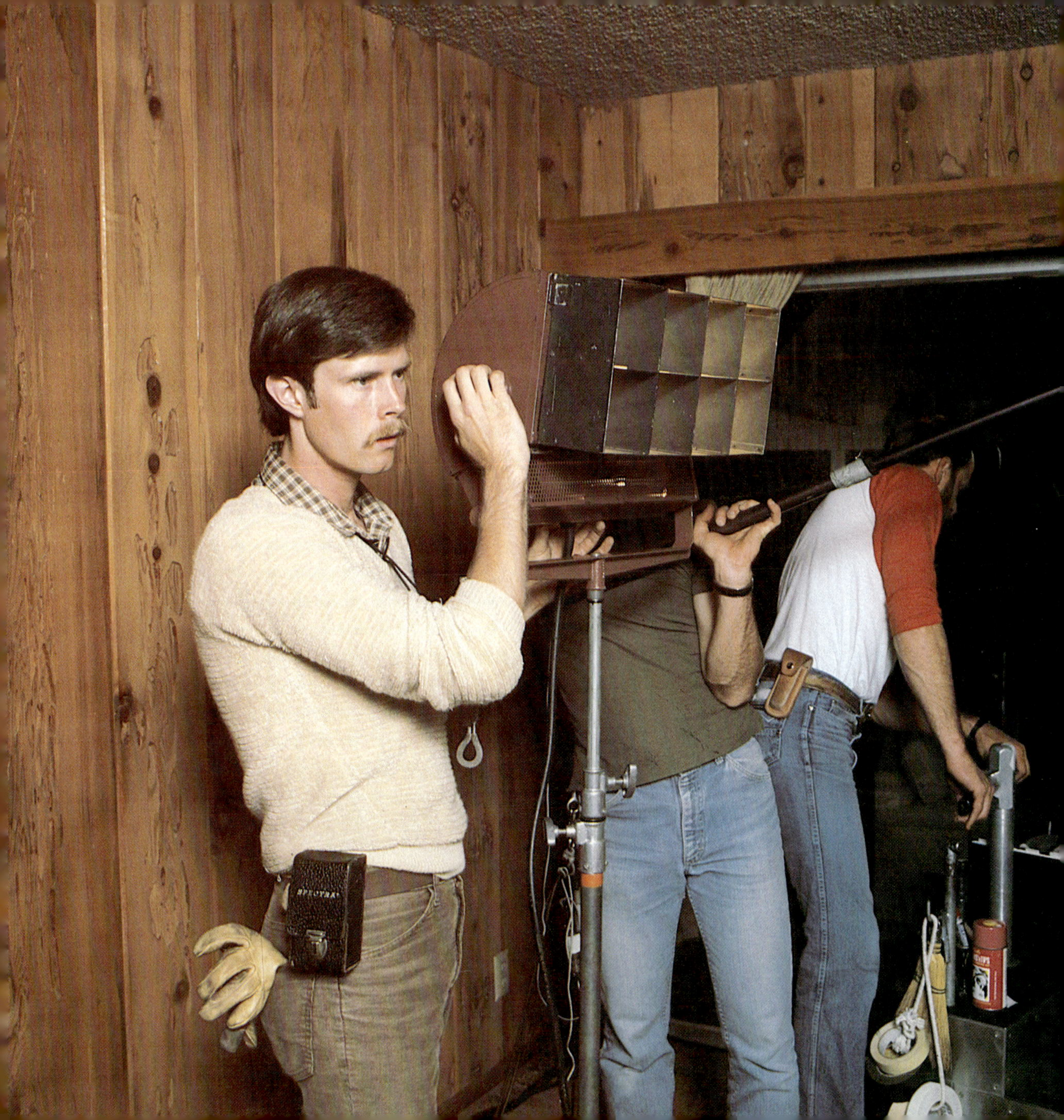

SOUND MIXER

The sound mixer is responsible for making sure the sounds in a movie are being properly recorded. While the actors talk, the sound mixer is busy adjusting the knobs on the mix unit, which controls the volume and pitch of the recordings. A sound mixer must be very familiar with different types of microphones.

Often the sound mixer is assisted by a *boom person.* The boom person holds a microphone on a very long pole over the head of the actor who is speaking. When filming takes place in a difficult location, the sound mixer may instead decide to use a tiny microphone, which the actor wears under his or her costume.

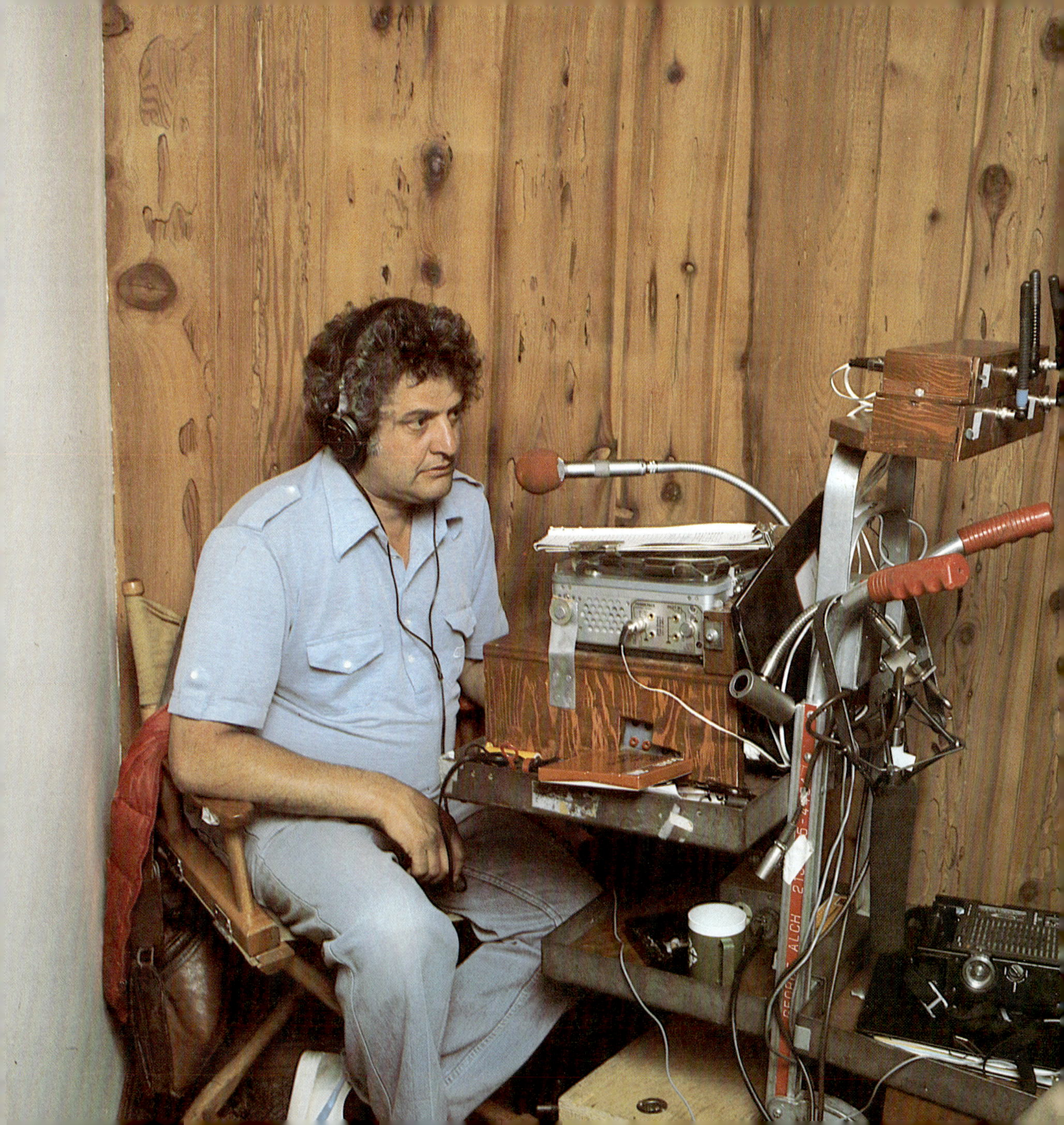
ALCH

LABORATORY TECHNICIAN

Laboratory technicians develop and print the film after each day's shooting. First they put the film in different chemicals to develop it. This process must be done in a room that is dark, or the film will be ruined. Next the technicians work in softly lit rooms, like the one in the picture, where they check the film as it is being printed. As the laboratory technicians watch thousands of feet of film pass through the machines, they check for scratches or changes in color.

Most laboratory technicians learn their work by training on the job. Sometimes a laboratory technician will look at over a mile of film in one day!

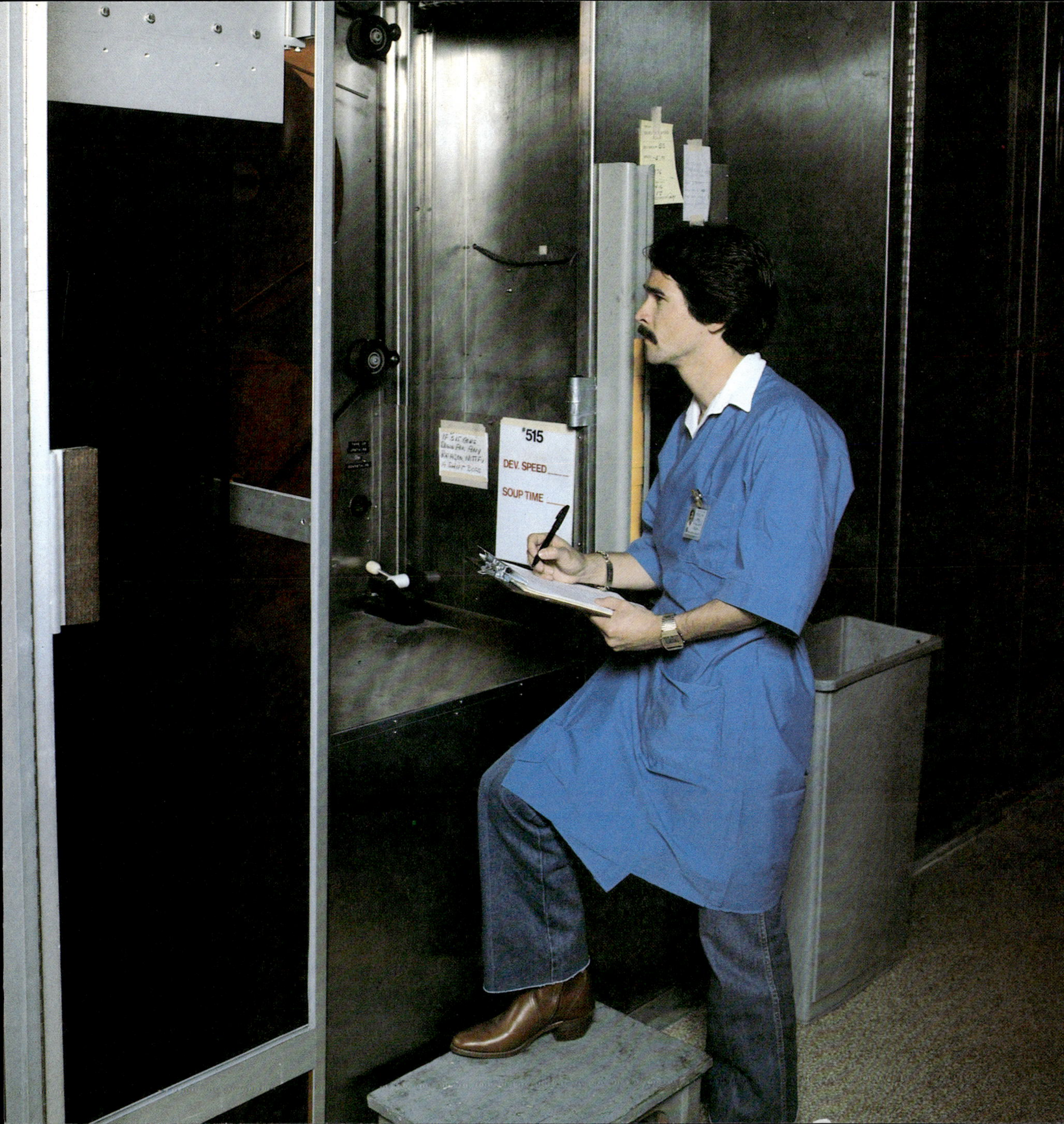
#515
DEV. SPEED
SOUP TIME

FILM EDITOR

When the director finishes filming a movie, all of the film is given to the film editor. A film editor decides which scenes will be put into the final version of the movie. To do this job, the editor and his or her assistant look at all of the pieces of film. Then they put the scenes in the right order according to the script.

To edit a film, an editor relies on many pieces of equipment, including a *moviola.* He or she uses the moviola to view the film footage along with the recorded sound. The editor chooses the scenes to be shown. Then he or she cuts the film with special scissors or blades and *splices,* or joins, the scenes together with clear tape. An editor will sometimes cut a scene several different ways, depending on the wishes of the director and producer.

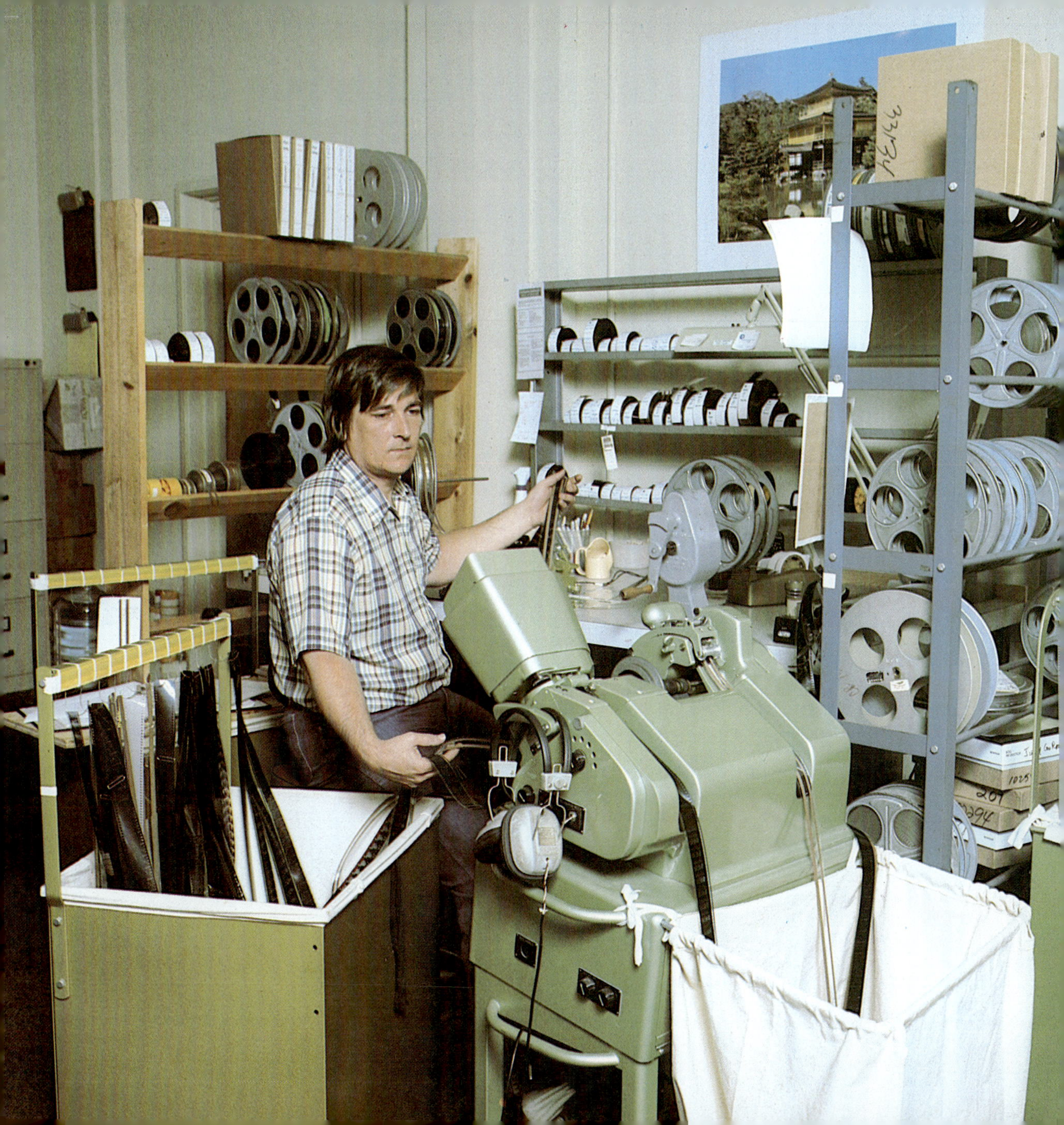

SOUND EFFECTS EDITOR

When you watch a movie, you may hear the sounds of cars rushing by, dogs barking, rain falling, or thunder crashing. These sounds are called *sound effects* because they give the effect of the barking dog or the falling rain without the dog or the rain actually being there. The person who makes all these sounds and fits them with the picture is called a sound effects editor.

Creating believable sound effects takes a lot of experimenting. In this picture, the sound effects editor is making the sound of a horse drinking at a stream. Sound effects editors work in a special studio called a *foley stage,* where all their tools are available.

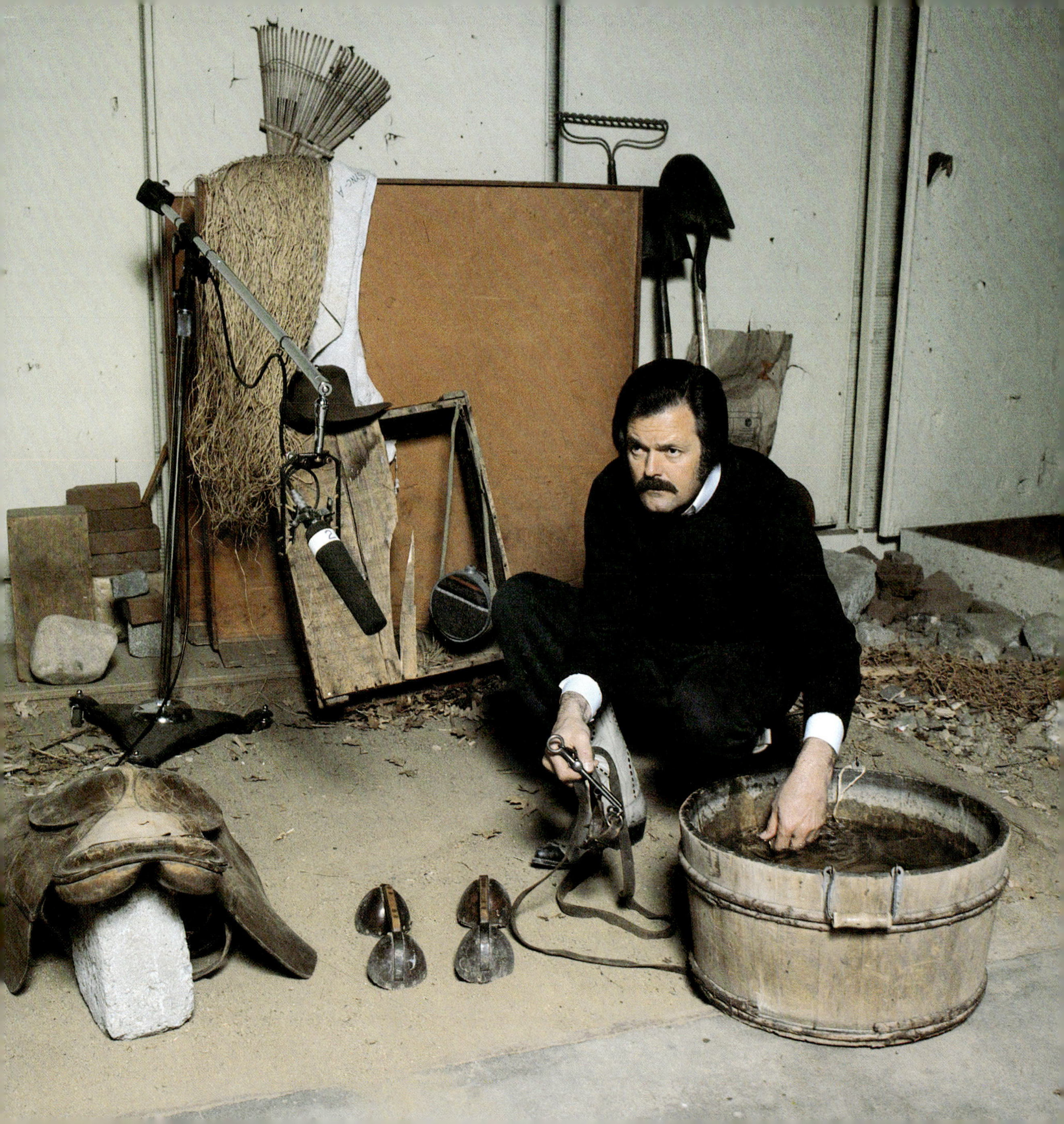

MAILROOM WORKER

One way to begin a career at a motion picture studio is to get a job in the mailroom. Mail must be delivered at least twice a day to every department on the studio lot. Since the studio is very large, mailroom workers use bicycles and electric carts to carry the mail.

They deliver mail to producers, screenwriters, property masters, film laboratory technicians, set designers, and everyone else who works at the studio. Seeing what these people do often helps mailroom workers decide which studio job they may want to have in the future.

You do not need much job experience to work in the mailroom, but you must be dependable, quick, and hard working.

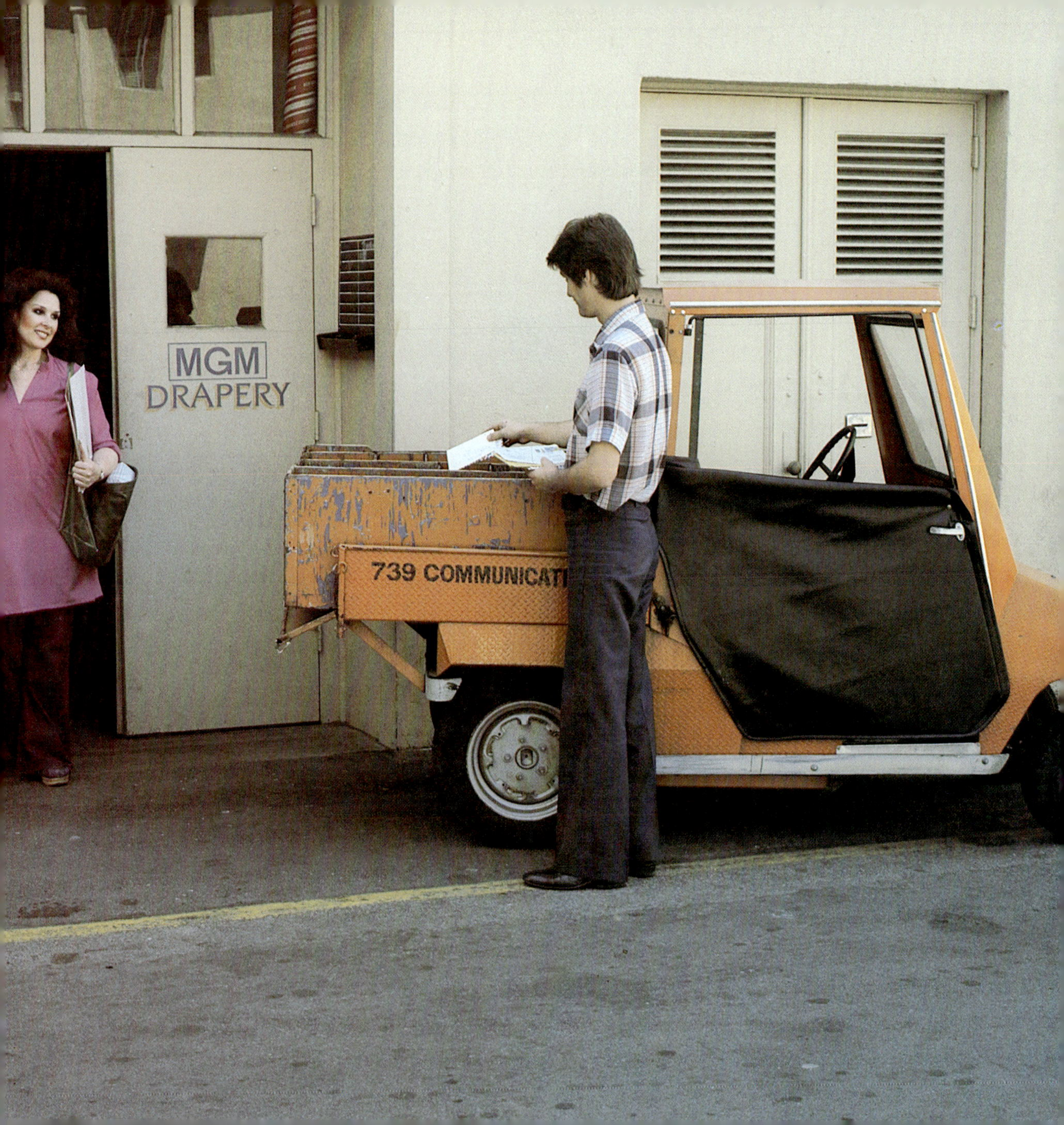
MGM
DRAPERY
739 COMMUNICATI

Movie Studio careers described in this book

Producer

Screenwriter

Production Manager

Set Designer

Property Master

Costume Designer

Director

Actor

Cinematographer

Chief Lighting Technician

Sound Mixer

Laboratory Technician

Film Editor

Sound Effects Editor

Mailroom Worker

The publisher would like to thank Nick Anderson and The Walz Johnson Company, Inc., Metro-Goldwyn-Mayer Film Company, and Darcie Denkert of MGM/UA Entertainment Corporation for their cooperation in the preparation of this book.

Lerner Publications Company
241 First Avenue North, Minneapolis, Minnesota 55401